GUITAR
Worship 2

Learn More Techniques and More Praise Songs — Book 2

by Garth Heckman

ISBN 978-1-4234-0737-9

HAL•LEONARD®
CORPORATION
7777 W. BLUEMOUND RD. P.O. BOX 13819 MILWAUKEE, WI 53213

In Australia contact:
Hal Leonard Australia Pty. Ltd.
4 Lentara Court
Cheltenham, Victoria, 3192 Australia
Email: ausadmin@halleonard.com.au

Visit Hal Leonard Online at
www.halleonard.com

Introduction

O Lord, open my lips,
And my mouth shall show forth Your praise.

—Psalm 51:15-17 (NKJV)

Welcome to the pages of *Guitar Worship Volume II*. If you have already purchased and practiced *Guitar Worship Volume I*, then you are on your way to better understanding the guitar and worship with Volume II.

To understand this book called *Guitar Worship*, you need to understand what worship is. The word *worship* comes from *worth ship*: something you ascribe worth to. If something has worth, you are willing to spend time on it, with it, and for it. If we want to truly be gifted in worship, we must give it the time, energy, and practice that it is worth. We must also use our talent to point to the worth of who God is. When we combine both of these, we begin to experience and enter into real *worth-ship*!

HOW TO USE THIS BOOK

- Make sure you have a solid understanding of *Volume I*. You might be confused on how to tune your guitar or on the different types of time signatures—if so, then go check out Volume I.

- Use this book immediately in your own worship time. Don't worry about getting through the book before you begin to use what you understand. Practice is the key—not just in a group setting, but also on your own time, in your own worship.

- Grab a friend and go through this book together. Your collective ideas and understanding will help you have a deeper understanding. You will both become more competent in your playing and in your understanding of this material.

- Use your electric guitar. If you don't have one, then use this book as an excuse to go out and buy one! The songs in this book are all arranged for an electric guitar sound. Hopefully, you already know that you can worship God with an electric guitar!

- Practice your guitar standing and sitting. You would be surprised at how different each position is when you only practice one way. Don't get caught off guard after sitting in your room practicing, only to find out that you can't play as well when you are standing up in church.

- DON'T PANIC! When we begin to talk about chords, intervals, diagrams, palm muting, tablature, and fingerings, new guitarists can break out in a cold sweat! Sometimes you can get so frustrated you want to throw the book down and just quit. If you do, go ahead and throw the book down, but pick up your guitar and just play, and relax. Then in a few minutes, pick the book back up and try it again. The guitar is meant to be fun first!

ABOUT THE CD

It's fun and rewarding to play worship guitar, and the accompanying CD will make your learning even more enjoyable. The best way to learn this material is to read and practice a while on your own, then listen to the CD. If there's something you don't understand the first time through, go back to the CD and listen again. Every musical example and song has been given a track number, so if you want to practice something again, you can find it right away.

First off, let's get in tune. The first track gives you the open strings of the guitar:

TRACK 1

⑥ ⑤ ④ ③ ② ①
E – A – D – G – B – E
low ⟵⟶ high

Contents

Movable Power Chords

Power Chords are the staple of many of today's great worship bands. They are basic chords, and easy to play. In just a few minutes of learning power chords, you could be writing out the greatest worship song ever on "Humility." There are a few ways to play power chords, and they are simple to move around the fretboard.

TWO OR THREE, IT'S UP TO ME!

A power chord can be played as a two-note chord or a three-note chord. Technically, they are not "full" chords, because most major and minor chords have at least three different notes— the 1st (or *root*), 5th, and 3rd (which can be major or minor)—and power chords only use the 1st and 5th intervals. What about three-note power chords? They still use only the 1st and 5th tones; the third note is just the root played an octave higher.

Typically, power chords are played based off the sixth (low E) and fifth (A) strings, but we will look at a few others later.

6th-String Root

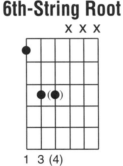

TRACK 2

5th-String Root

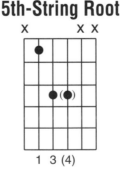

TRACK 3

Notice that each power chord is based off the root note played by your first (or "pointer") finger. Your first finger "points" to the root, which gives your power chord its name. By learning the names of the notes across the fifth and sixth strings, you learn dozens of power chords and chord placements.

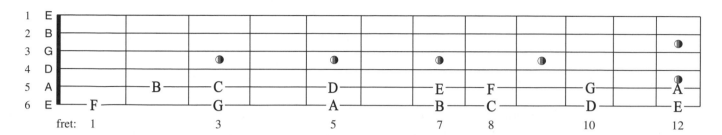

POWER PRAISE

Try these examples using two-note power chords. Refer to the fretboard diagram for your root notes. Notice that power chords are labeled with the suffix "5." Let's use all downstrokes for these.

TRACK 4

I Praise You in the dark - ness, I Praise You in the light. I

Praise You for your right - eous-ness, I Praise You for Your might.___

TRACK 5

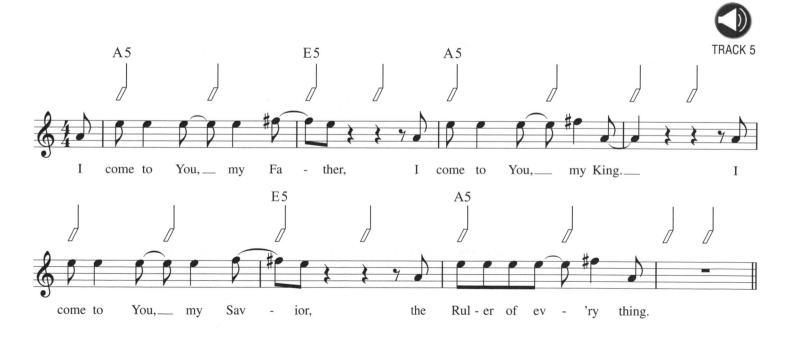

I come to You,___ my Fa - ther, I come to You,___ my King.___ I

come to You,___ my Sav - ior, the Rul - er of ev - 'ry thing.

5

PICKUP NOTES

Did you notice that the vocals started before the first measure in the previous examples? To show this we use a *pickup measure*—a partial measure that comes at the beginning of a song. For the previous two examples, just count "one–and–two–and–three–and–four," and start singing on the "and" of beat 4.

I PROMISED YOU THREE

As you play these *three-note power chords,* notice that they are a little more thick and spicy sounding. This is due to the added root note one octave higher. So simply speaking, you have a three-note chord that's really only made up of two *different* notes.

TRACK 6

My King, my Lord, my King, my Con - quer - or. _____

My King, my Lord, my Rul - er of ev - 'ry - thing. _____

TRACK 7

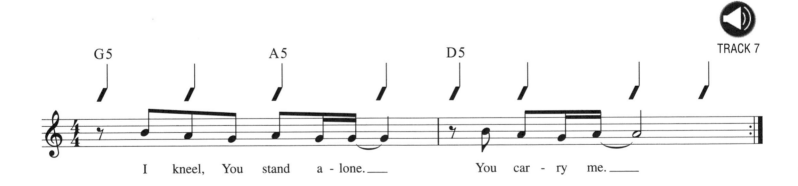

I kneel, You stand a - lone. _____ You car - ry me. _____

SIXTEENTH NOTES

If you really want to make a joyful noise unto the Lord, try *sixteenth* notes. These happen at double the speed of eighth notes.

Two sixteenth notes equal one eighth note; four sixteenth notes equal one quarter note. And below is the whole diagram to better understand how it all falls into place.

Notice that a sixteenth note has two flags on it, unlike an eighth note which has only one. When sixteenth notes are placed together, they have just two big beams across the tops of the notes.

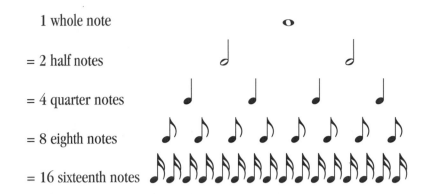

The best way to play these is by using a simple drummer's trick. You count each note giving each beat a value of four, like this:

TRACK 8

1 - e - & - a, 2 - e - & - a, 3 - e - & - a, 4 - e - & - a

MUTE IT!

Palm muting is a great way to add nuances to your song that sometimes help emphasize a part you want to stand out. How do you do it? Simply rest your palm or the side of your picking hand on the strings lightly while you play. Do this right at the point where the strings meet the bridge—and don't push too hard, or you'll change the pitch. This can give you a percussive sound that can add variety to your songs. Use this whenever you see the abbreviation "P.M."

TRACK 9

PROGRAM YOUR DOME WITH THE 'NOME!

Use a metronome to learn to keep time when playing sixteenth notes. If you don't have one, it can be picked up at any music store and is usually pretty inexpensive. It will help you keep from rushing and getting sloppy. Start out at a slow tempo, and play four even notes for every beat of the metronome. Try the example above with the metronome first, then without.

This example is played with a combination of eighth and sixteenth notes. You can count the part like, "1–&–a, 2–&–a, 3–&–a, 4–&–a." Play with a "down, down–up" pattern.

JOHN 3:16TH NOTES

TRACK 10

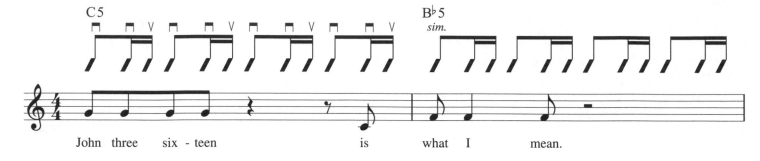

John three six-teen is what I mean.

Took all my sins, and now I'm clean.

Let's play this next one with straight alternate picking ("down, up, down, up," etc.). Notice the first and second endings—remember those from the *Volume I* book? Play through the first ending, then go back to the first repeat sign. The second time through, skip the first ending and play the second. The "Double-time feel" indicates that, although you're strumming sixteenth notes, they'll feel like eighth notes because the drums are playing a beat that's twice as fast as normal.

TRACK 11

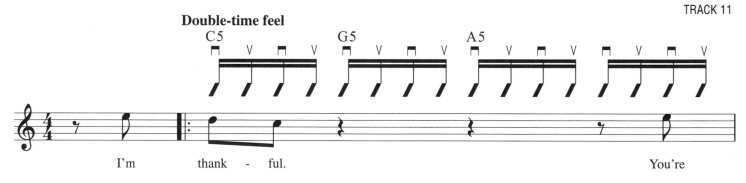

I'm thank-ful. You're

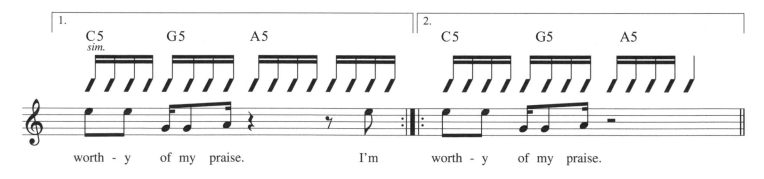

worth-y of my praise. I'm worth-y of my praise.

WHAT'S THE BUZZ?

When playing the power chord rooted on the fifth string, you may get a little buzz going on the sixth string. To help keep that sixth string from doing its own thing, you can use the tip of your first finger to rest slightly into (not on top of) the string, touching it just enough to keep it quiet.

ACCENT THAT THING!

You can add even more variety by following the *accent marks* (>). Accent marks show you where to play a note a little louder then the others. Combine this with some palm muting for a needed breath of fresh air in your playing. The "Half-time feel" direction is basically the opposite of the "Double-time feel" direction we saw earlier.

WONDROUS MAKER

TRACK 12

Barre Chords

Barre chords are movable chord positions that will open up the neck of the guitar to a new world of possibilities. Playing the major and minor patterns up and down the neck will be simple once you learn a few of the more common shapes. The most common barre chords are based on four basic open chord positions: E, Em, A, and Am.

Let's first strengthen that hand before we tackle a full barre chord. Remember, this is where many guitarists stop learning. The chords can seem difficult to learn at first, but there is a secret that great guitarists have learned—it's called PRACTICE. Maybe that's not the secret you were hoping for, but it works nonetheless. So don't give up!

THE SIMPLE FULL BARRE

Use the index (pointer) finger of your fret hand to press firmly down on all the strings. Flatten it out, so that all strings are covered evenly. Once this is achieved, play each string separately to make sure none are muted or buzzing.

Make sure your thumb is pressing directly behind the neck of the guitar, as if you were trying to pinch through the neck.

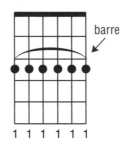

TRACK 13

Note: it may help to slightly twist your wrist to the outside of the guitar (toward the headstock) so that your index finger is pressing with more of the side of the finger.

FORM I MAJOR BARRE CHORDS

Form I is based on the E major open-position chord. The chord shape is the same but with a slight change in fingering, and the index finger now barres the shape. This shape is used to play barre chords up and down the neck, using the sixth string as your root position.

Practice first playing an open E chord with your second, third, and fourth fingers. Rest your index finger over the nut without pressing.

E

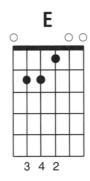

3 4 2

TRACK 14

Now move your fingers up one fret, and place your index finger across all six strings at the first fret, pressing firmly. This produces a barre chord.

F barre

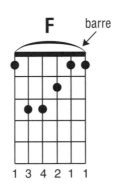

1 3 4 2 1 1

TRACK 15

Try strumming all six strings to make sure each one is heard clearly. This first barre chord is an F major, based off of its root note on the sixth string, first fret.

By moving this shape up the neck of the guitar, you can play that barre chord on almost every fret. In fact, you may find that playing a barre chord is a little easier moving it further up the neck. Remember, as you slide your hand up, to keep your technique in check; first, play each string separately to check for buzzes and muted strings.

ISN'T IT AMAZING

TRACK 16

Half-time feel

Is-n't it a - maz-ing; Your love?___

Play 3 times

FORM I MINOR BARRE CHORDS

Let's try a form I minor chord! This is a barred form of an open-position E minor. The same goes for fingering, but be careful again about unwanted buzzing!

Fm

1 3 4 1 1 1

TRACK 17

FORM II MAJOR BARRE CHORDS

The form II major barre chord is based on the open-position A major chord. Notice that the shape is the same, but with a slight change in fingering, and the index finger now barres the shape. This shape is used to play barre chords up and down the neck using the fifth string as your root position.

Practice playing an open A chord with your third finger, using it to barre all three strings in the A major chord. Rest your index finger over the nut without pressing.

A

X ○ ○

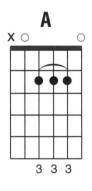

3 3 3

TRACK 18

Once this feels comfortable, you can attempt form II. Move your fingers up one fret and place your index finger across the first fret. Press firmly. This produces a barre chord.

A♯(B♭)

X

1 3 3 3 1

TRACK 19

Try strumming all five fretted strings to see if each one is heard clearly and at an even volume. This barre chord is a B♭ major, based on its root note on the fifth string, first fret.

Note: It is sometimes hard to play the five strings in form II without playing the low E. One way to mute that string is to let the tip of your first finger rest into (not on top of) that string while playing the other five strings in the chord.

WHAT ABOUT THE HIGH E STRING?

It can be a trick to barre three strings with your third finger without muting the high E string. This takes time and practice. Try using just your third finger on a few barre chords, and try to keep the high E sounding clearly. It may help to place your third finger at different spots (vertically) in order to provide clearance for the first string.

Try this example using both forms of major barre chords.

OUT OF THE TOMB AND INTO MY HEART

TRACK 20

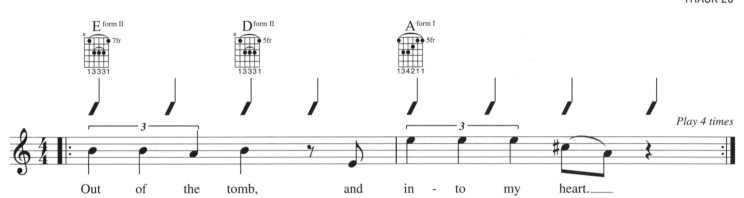

Out of the tomb, and in - to my heart._____

Play 4 times

FORM II MINOR BARRE CHORDS

Now that you have successfully completed Form II major chords, lets take a stab at Form II minor positions. Try using just your second, third, and fourth fingers to fret an open-position A minor chord, with your index finger resting on the nut.

Am

TRACK 21

Once you feel comfortable playing this, slide your hand up one fret and press your first finger down on fret 1.

A♯m(B♭m)

TRACK 22

FINGER LOOK'N' GOOD!

You may have to practice a little extra to transition from Form I to Form II, while bouncing around from one fret to another... but, with practice it gets easier and easier. Hang in there and soon it will be finger look'n' good! Practice these chords to start learning how to transition with greater ease.

G

C

Dm

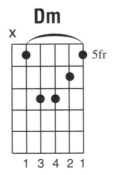

5fr

TRACK 23

Chords and Progressions

WHAT MAKES A CHORD?

We have been playing chords for a while now, but maybe you are still asking yourself, "What makes a chord?" It's simple: two cups of sugar, a cup of flour... OK, maybe it is a little more detailed than that. A traditional chord is simply three or more notes played simultaneously. (The exception, as you've seen, is a two-note power chord.) When a group of chords are played in a song, they are the foundation or the "harmony" on which you then build the melody.

WHAT ARE THE INGREDIENTS?

Using the C major chord as our example, let's take a closer look at what makes up the ingredients in the two most common chord types.

Chord Type	Ingredients	Notes in Chord	Chord Symbol
Major	1–3–5	C–E–G	C
Minor	1–♭3–5	C–E♭–G	Cm

MAJOR, MINOR—WHAT DO THEY SOUND LIKE?

It's the power of 3! As you can see, the immediate difference between the major and minor chord is the "3," or 3rd interval. In a minor chord it is *flattened*; this is what makes the minor chord sound "sad." Hey, wouldn't you be sad if you were flattened? The minor chord is fundamental to many worship choruses, because it adds that feeling of brokenness.

Notice the difference when playing an A major chord, compared to A minor:

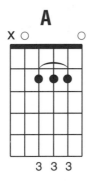

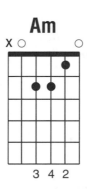

TRACK 24

But which chord works? There can be a lot of confusion regarding what chords to use and not to use when writing music. It is important to know why each chord has the major or minor value that it has. That's why there's the *diatonic progression*. Don't let the big new word scare you; it's pretty simple to understand. The diatonic breakdown always starts with the scale. Read on...

DIATONIC CHORD PROGRESSIONS

Let's look at the C major scale. If you play each note as a full chord, it breaks down into a formula of major and minor chords. This formula is used in every major key.

Scale degree	1	2	3	4	5	6	7
Note/chord root	C	D	E	F	G	A	B
Chord type	major	minor	minor	major	major	minor	diminished

Notice the formula: major, minor, minor, major, major, minor, diminished. (We'll talk more about diminished chords later.)

Let's look at this practically. If you simply wanted to know what chords work when writing a song in the key of C, they are simply this: C major, D minor, E minor, F major, G major, A minor, and B diminished. So even if you mixed these chords up and played them randomly, they would sound pretty good together and none of them would clash. There is more to song writing than simply this, but it doesn't get much harder than that. Simple, huh?

Let's look at another key, G. The G major scale has one sharp note, F♯. This F♯ note does not change value just because it's a sharp note, so the formula stays the same as it was for C major.

Scale degree	1	2	3	4	5	6	7
Note/chord root	G	A	B	C	D	E	F♯
Chord type	major	minor	minor	major	major	minor	diminished

This means that if you want to write a song in the Key of G, you can use any of these chords: G major, A minor, B minor, C major, D major, E minor, and F♯ diminished. By keeping the above formula, you can play these chords in any order and they will sound good together.

COMMON KEYS

Here are the common guitar keys and the diatonic breakdown of each:

Key	1 major	2 minor	3 minor	4 major	5 major	6 minor	7 diminished
C	C	Dm	Em	F	G	Am	B°
G	G	Am	Bm	C	D	Em	F♯°
D	D	Em	F♯m	G	A	Bm	C♯°
A	A	Bm	C♯m	D	E	F♯m	G♯°
E	E	F♯m	G♯m	A	B	C♯m	D♯°

BEYOND THE DIATONIC WORLD

Though the diatonic chord formula always works and is a safe method for writing songs, it's certainly not a hard and fast rule! In other words, you'll often see other chords in a song that's in the key of G than the seven listed above. These chords are called *non-diatonic* chords, and though the subject is too big to tackle here, it's certainly worth investigating further.

Now try these songs in the keys of G, A, and C:

SALVATION IS YOURS

TRACK 25

Play 4 times

Sal - va - tion is Yours,___ my King.___

*Non-diatonic chord

WRITE YOUR OWN LYRICS!

TRACK 26

Half-time feel

I CALL ON YOU NOW

TRACK 27

Come quick - ly, come soft ly, come to me now.___

Come quick - ly, come soft - ly, I call on You now.___

FINDING A SONG'S KEY

Finding the key of a piece of music can be frustrating unless you understand the formula. The easiest way to find the key of a song is to look for the two major chords that are next to each other (the 4 and 5 in the formula) in a scale. In the key of C, these would be F major and G major; in the key of A, it would be D major and E major; in the key of D, it would be G major and A major.

When you find the 4 and 5 (the two majors) in a piece of music, you simply count backwards to the root. For example: G major and A major are your 4 and 5. Now, count backwards: A major (5), G major (4), F♯ minor (3), E minor (2), D major (1 or the root "key").

Here are some examples you can try.

The chord progression (or the song) includes the following chords; what is the key?

1.	Am	G	Em	F	=	Key: _____
2.	Em	D	G	A	=	Key: _____
3.	A	D	C♯m	E	=	Key: _____

Answers: 1. Key of C

2. Key of D*

3. Key of A

*This one may have been tricky. Remember that the scale has seven notes and continually repeats itself. Therefore, when you get to G in a scale, it continues on up to A to the end of the scale. So in the key of D, the 4 and 5 are G and A. Make sure you are aware of this as you look at chords in music.

Song Structure

Now, you might still be wondering about how you actually *write* a worship song. Great question, and here is hopefully the right answer. First, remember that the best worship song is written from a pure heart and reflects an element or characteristic of who God is. That said, there is a basic structure to modern worship songwriting. You know the chords, and you now know the diatonic structure in which they are used, so let's look into the specifics.

Every song can be looked at as a house. There are certain foundations that you can begin to work with. But, everyone likes his or her house a little different. So if you work on the foundation principles, in time you can add your own nuances to make it your "dream house." Here are the basic parts of one possible foundation.

- **Intro:** Usually short, and based on the chords within the verse, this may be played by one instrument or the whole band.

- **Verse:** Typically four lines; to keep it simple, stick with 4/4 time.

- **Verse 2:** Builds off of the same theme as verse one with four lines.

- **Chorus:** Four lines (usually) that express or explain the verses in light of worship.

- **Verse Three:** Four lines that now wrap up the concept of the chorus.

- **Chorus:** Same as above.

- **Instrumental Lead:** This is not a typical part of a worship song, but can be used sparsely in your writing at times to add some variety.

- **Bridge:** Think of the bridge as an interlude. It often is a point of reflection in a worship song, with no lyrics (though it certainly can have lyrics).

- **Chorus:** Sing it twice this time.

- **Ending:** Characteristically, it is based on the chorus and may either fade or end abruptly according to the mood of the song.

Note: This is how you typically write a basic worship song, but in performance it may take a totally different shape. You may feel like the mood of the worship experience is leading you to play the chorus four times instead of once or twice. You also may find other nuances, like playing the bridge longer than the typical length. You must learn to read the crowd and listen to what you feel God wants you to do during the worship experience.

Arpeggios

An *arpeggio* is a chord played one note at a time. For example, a C chord is made up of the notes C, E, and G (or the 1, 3, and 5 of the scale). To play an arpeggio, one would play those notes. It can be more complicated than this, but for now that's all you need to know. The idea is to play each note separately rather then strum the chord as a whole.

Arpeggiated chords are simply chords that are played note-by-note in a singular fashion. Each string has its own distinguishable sound, rather than a fully strummed chord. Arpeggiated chords are usually played from lowest to highest, but not always. Below are some simple examples using open-position chords—just hold the chords and pick one note at a time.

RHYTHM TAB

To show the arpeggios, we're using a style of notation called *tablature*, or *tab*. This is a diagram of the strings that shows you what frets to play on each string. Better yet, this is *rhythm tab*, which shows you the length of the notes you're playing as well.

TRACK 28

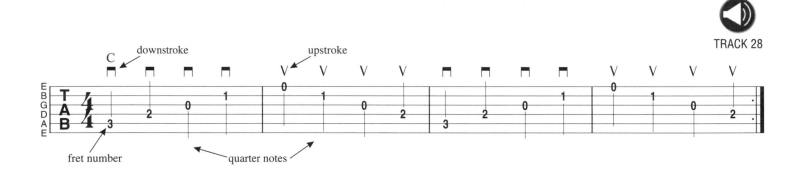

Remember the 3/4 time signature? Each measure has three quarter notes instead of four.

TRACK 29

TRACK 30

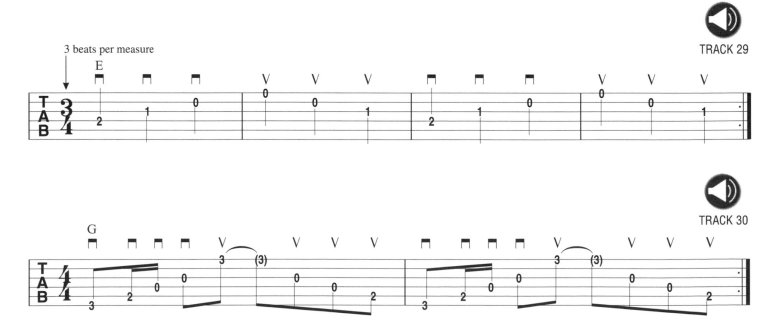

Here are some simple song examples using arpeggiated chords.

TRACK 31

TRACK 32

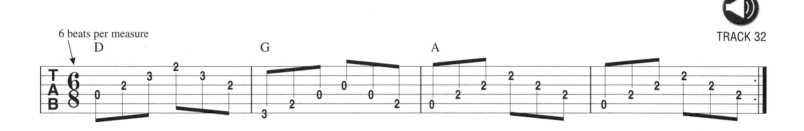

Notice the difference in sound and feeling when you arpeggiate a chord rather than strum it.

Now let's try a song using arpeggiated barre chords.

COME, GLORIOUS LORD

TRACK 33

Many times, a song will incorporate strummed parts and arpeggiated versions of the same chords to add a new depth and feeling—a simple technique that can be very effective in adding a verse, bridge, or chorus without having to use any new chords. Listen to this next example and notice the difference.

RECEIVE ME NOW

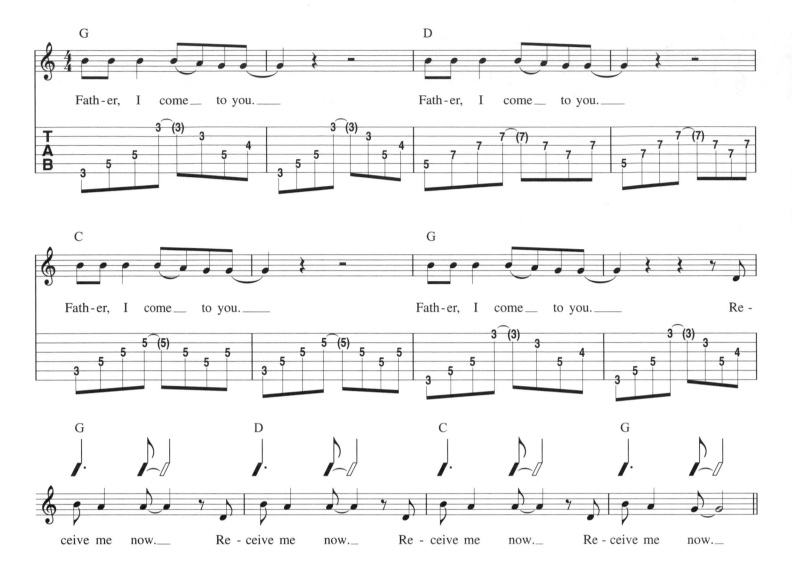

See if you can take a simple chord progression you have already written, and add arpeggios to it. You will be surprised at how it may fit nicely as a bridge, verse, or chorus.

Understanding Scales

Now is the time to put a frame around the picture we have painted so far in this book. Everything in these pages is based simply on the understanding of scales within our Western thinking of music. (No, I am not talking about country music!) Chords, leads, and (as we've seen) song structure are all framed by the almighty scale.

Scales are simply notes that are played individually, based off of our twelve-tone musical library. (This library has only twelve books, and each book is a tone.) Those twelve tones are:

A	A#/B♭	B	C	C#/D♭	D	D#/E♭	E	F	F#/G♭	G	G#/A♭

Sometimes two notes in the scale—such as C# and D♭—are the same note, but have two different names. They are called *enharmonics*.

A, B, C, D, E, F, and G are *natural* tones, or the "white keys" on the piano. A# or B♭, C# or D♭, D# or E♭, F# or G♭, and G# or A♭ are the *accidentals*, or the "black keys" on the piano.

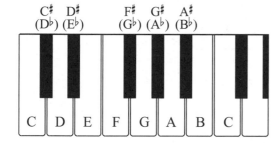

Notice that there are no sharps or flats between B and C, or E and F. These are the places where you see two white keys together on the keyboard.

The major scale is made up of seven notes from our twelve-tone musical library. The key of that scale can be based off any of those twelve tones. The scale is what we use as the foundation of our melody, solo, or riff.

BREAK IT DOWN FOR ME!

Let's simplify it this way: out of the twelve tones, let's pick a note... OK, C it is. Now let's look at the C major scale. (Remember, all major scales have seven notes.) The notes that make up that scale are based on some simple *steps* (literally, steps!) and *half steps*.

Whole step – whole step – half step – whole step – whole step – whole step – half step

So if you looked at the keyboard, you would see the C scale take on this shape: C (W) to D (W) to E (H) to F (W) to G (W) to A (W) to B (H) back to C.

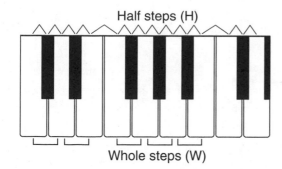

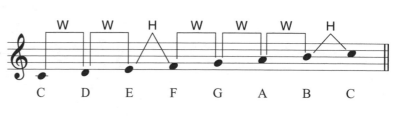

Now let's look at another tone out of the twelve-note musical library. Let's pick D to build our next scale.

D (W) to E (W) to F♯ (H) to G (W) to A (W) to B (W) to C♯ (H) back to D

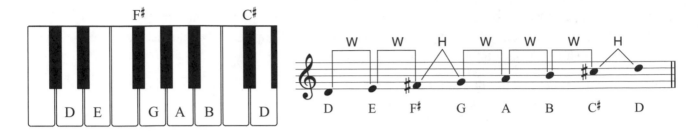

Notice that the sharp notes fall on the black keys, and these share the enharmonic names of their flat counterparts.

Remember: on the guitar, a half step (H) is one fret to the next, and a whole step (W) is two frets.

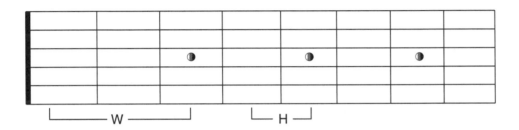

WHAT'S THE KEY?

The key of a piece of music is based off of the scale. If a piece of music is in the key of B, we understand that the chords are based off of the B scale—and so is its solo, melody, and any riffs you come up with for that song.

Remember: scales are notes played singularly, and chords are the notes based off each of the degrees in that scale (diatonic progression), played simultaneously.

Let's look at playing a simple A major scale on the guitar, and then building a five-note riff from that scale.

TRACK 35

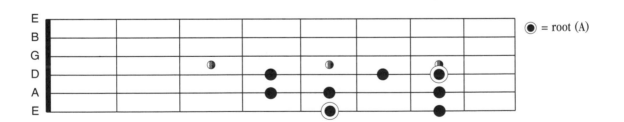

⊚ = root (A)

TRACK 36

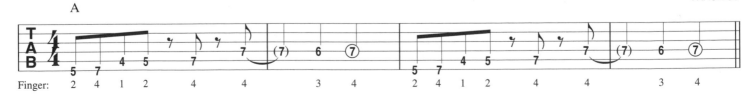

THE MINOR PENTATONIC SCALE

Let's look at one of the building blocks of good soloing. It is the *minor pentatonic scale*, and it is based off of five tones from our musical library. This is an easy scale to learn and can be used in all styles of music.

Box 1

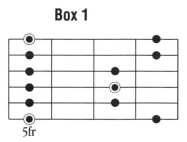

Notice the root note of the scale (circled). This root is where you "anchor" your scale position for the key you are playing in (i.e., if you are playing in the key of A, you would move your pattern to where your root note is—the fifth fret).

A great way to fill out an upbeat worship song is with some simple soloing. The most common scale in Western music is the pentatonic scale ("penta" meaning five, and "tonic" meaning tone or note). The minor pentatonic scale is comprised of the intervals 1–♭3–4–5–♭7. The major and minor pentatonic scale are the foundation for soloing in blues, rock, country, and even jazz. One must learn this scale and the five boxes it is contained in. The good news, as with any scale, is that these boxes can be moved to any key. So if you learn these five, you essentially have learned them in all keys on the guitar. Here they are presented in the key of A minor:

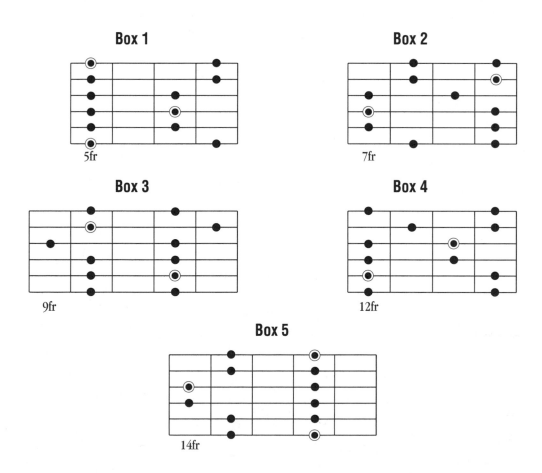

As with any scale, make sure you pick each string with an even tempo and use an alternate picking sequence.

Try these simple pentatonic exercises and riffs using alternate picking.

This first exercise is to try to play from the first box, low to high and back again, then slide up to the second box and play it the same. Try to do this seamlessly and in an even tempo.

TRACK 37

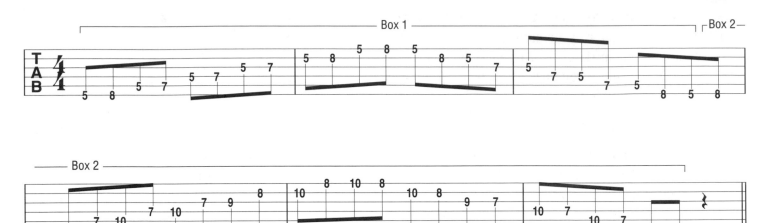

This time we will start by going up the first box, shift up and descend on the second, then continue through all five boxes, finally ending up at the high octave position of box 1.

TRACK 38

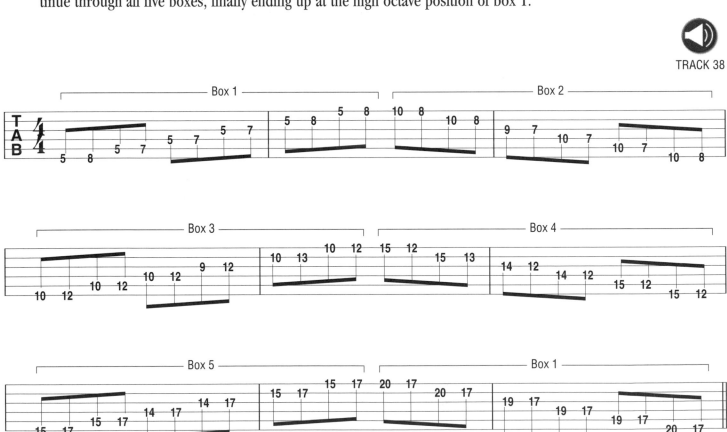

Now that you have started to master this, let's try a basic minor pentatonic riff.

REMEMBER THE METRONOME?

Now, before you pick up any bad habits while practicing scales, you must understand the importance of using a metronome. You will never achieve your full potential if you don't have one—and trust me, your band will thank you!

PLAYING OVER I–IV–V PROGRESSIONS

The most common chord progression in history is the *I–IV–V* progression. You must be comfortable playing this if you want to become a well-rounded musician. Naturally, it's made up of three chords from the diatonic progression—I, IV, and V—but not necessarily in that order. Let's try a few examples, and then maybe we will even solo over a few.

SWING IT!

The following example is played with a *shuffle* or *swing feel*, in which a pair of eighth notes is played as a long and short note, more like a heartbeat. Listen and notice the difference.

TELL THE WORLD

TRACK 40

DARK, DARK NIGHT

Dark dark night___ in the mid-dle of the day.___

Je-sus on the cross, my sin to pay.___

The mid-dle of e - vil,

with a love so strong.___ I had to look a - way. It was right, but it was oh, so___ wrong.___

Now moving to the root of each example, you can play some of those pentatonic riffs you already learned over these progressions—i.e., if you're playing over "Tell the World," start with the fifth-fret pentatonic box 1. Next, try it in the other two chord progressions.

NOTES ON THE NECK

While it is not completely necessary to memorize all the notes on the neck to play the guitar effectively, you will find it very helpful. There are a few ways to do this; let's look at a few.

This first example is simply knowing the basic root and the major octaves found within a few frets of each. Here, the root and octaves of A are shown in circles.

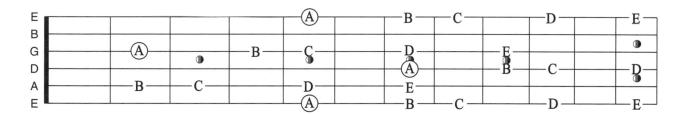

Notice that if you know the first few intervals of the major scale, you can piece together the other notes within those strings on adjacent strings. Look to the octaves within each key, and you can quickly memorize the intervals based off of the root. Try to build intervals off the root and octaves of the other notes: B, C, and D.

The next example is simply memorizing the notes one string at a time. This may seem tedious, but in time it gets easy, and you will be surprised at how well you can know the complete fretboard in only a few days of practice.

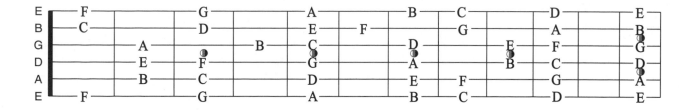

More Chords

Here are a few other basic and unusual chords that can help you break out of a rut in your playing.

First, some power chords that go beyond the basic power chords you used before. These can add some spice to your louder praise and worship songs.

G#5

TRACK 43

C#5

TRACK 44

D#5

TRACK 45

G#5

X X X

1 4 4

TRACK 46

Here are some three-note chords that are thinner sounding and can cut through a song to give some great ambiance with the right effects.

B

X X X

3 4 1

TRACK 47

E

X X X

1 3 2

TRACK 48

F

X X X

2 1 1

TRACK 49

Bm

x x x

3 2 1

TRACK 50

Em

x x x

2 3 1

TRACK 51

Fm

x x x

1 1 1

TRACK 52

"JUST SO YOU KNOW" CHORDS

Every now and then you will pick up some worship music and see some chords that are not often seen, but need to be known.

Dsus4

TRACK 53

Dsus2

TRACK 54

Asus4

TRACK 55

Asus2

TRACK 56

Esus4

TRACK 57

Em(add9)

TRACK 58

Fmaj7

TRACK 59

Cmaj7

TRACK 60

Cadd9

TRACK 61

Heart of a Worship Leader

Now you have learned notes, chords, arpeggios, and even a few licks for your songs. What is most important? I believe that as a worship leader you must practice your instrument, but I also believe you must practice living a life of worship. Too often we hang our egos on how well we play or how many songs we have written—but this is not what worship is about. A good question to ask yourself before you lead worship is simply, "Do I want people to remember me, or the God I represent?" If you can't answer that question correctly, then maybe you should continue to practice living the life of a worshiper and then, later, try the lifestyle of a worship leader.

To me there can be no greater joy than to see people enjoy worshiping God, and at the same time there is no greater sadness to God than to see people miss him and only see the worship leader. May your prayer be the same as we see in Psalm 51:

O Lord, open my lips,
And my mouth shall show forth Your praise.
For You do not desire sacrifice, or else I would give it;
You do not delight in burnt offering.
The sacrifices of God are a broken spirit,
A broken and a contrite heart—
These, O God, You will not despise.

> —Psalm 51:15-17 (NKJV)

Praise on!

Garth Heckman

And just in case you are all fired up to write a song, but can't find the lyrics, you can practice on this one!

VERSE

Your bonds are my delight
Your words are my light
I cast my cares on your throne
I worship you alone

CHORUS

I come to you today
Eternity is yours to see
You saw my steps all the way
You're always there for me

Mix and match it, make it yours! Enjoy!

christian**guitar**songbooks